LEVEL 3

Mars

Elizabeth Carney

NATIONAL GEOGRAPHIC

Washington, D.C.

For Ellie: May you grow up to find the
solar system at your fingertips. —E. C.

The publisher and author gratefully acknowledge the expert review
of this book by Kirsten Siebach of the California Institute of Technology.

Paperback ISBN: 978-1-4263-1747-7
Reinforced library edition ISBN: 978-1-4263-1748-4

Book design by YAY! Design

cover, JPL/Cornell University/NASA; 1, David Aguilar/NGS; 2, NASA-JPL/Science Faction/Corbis; 4-5, JPL/Cornell/NASA; 5 (UP),
David Aguilar/NGS; 6 (LE), David Aguilar/NGS; 6 (RT), David Aguilar/NGS; 8-9, Babak Tafreshi/National Geographic Creative;
9 (LO), DeAgostini/G. Dagli Orti/Getty Images; 10 (UP), upsidedowndog/iStockphoto; 10 (LO), design56/Shutterstock; 11, Science
Source; 13, IBMP, Oleg Voloshin, HO/AP Images; 14-15, Detlev van Ravenswaay/Science Source; 16-17, JPL/Cornell/NASA; 16 (UP),
Dr. Mark Garlick; 16 (LO), Stocktrek Images, Inc./Alamy; 17 (UP), Sumikophoto/Shutterstock; 17 (CTR), Zeljko Radojko/Shutterstock;
17 (LO), Dimitri Vervitsiotis/Digital Vision/Getty Images; 19 (UP), JPL-Caltech/Univ. of Arizona/NASA; 19 (LO), Kees Veenenbos/Sci-
ence Source; 20 (LE), NASA; 20 (RT), NASA; 21 (UPLE), JPL-Caltech/NASA; 21 (UPRT), JPL/Cornell University, Maas Digital LLC/NASA;
21 (CTR), JPL/NASA; 21 (LO), JPL-Caltech/NASA; 22, NASA; 23, JPL-Caltech/NASA; 25, JPL-Caltech/NASA; 26, Brian Van Der Brug/Los
Angeles Times/MCT/ZUMAPRESS.com; 27 (UP), Damian Dovarganes/AP Images; 27 (LO), Damian Dovarganes/AP Images; 29, Red
Huber/MCT/ZUMAPRESS.com; 30-31, Ruaridh Stewart/ZUMAPRESS.com; 32, Robyn Beck/AFP/Getty Images; 33 (LE), Rex Features/AP
Images; 33 (UPRT), Rex Features/AP Images; 33 (CTR RT), Rex Features/AP Images; 33 (LORT), Rex Features/AP Images; 35, NASA/UPI/
Newscom; 36-37, Stephan Morrel/National Geographic Creative; 38-39, Stephan Morrel/National Geographic Creative; 41 (UPLE),
SSPL/Getty Images; 41 (UPRT), Universal/Kobal Collection; 41 (LOLE), K.J. Historical/Corbis; 41 (LORT), B. Speckart/Shutterstock; 42,
Kim Kulish/Corbis; 43, Steve Gschmeissner/SPL/Getty Images; 44 (UP), David Aguilar/NGS; 44 (CTR), JPL-Caltech/NASA; 44 (LO),
David Aguilar/NGS; 45 (UP-1), Pablo Hidalgo/Shutterstock; 45 (UP-2), Preto Perola/Shutterstock; 45 (UP-3), Ewa Studio/Shutter-
stock; 45 (UP-4), S.Borisov/Shutterstock; 45 (CTR RT), NASA; 45 (CTR LE), NASA; 45 (LO), Michael Stravato/AP Images; 46 (UPRT),
Julian Love/AWL Images RM/Getty Images; 46 (CTR LE), Cheryl Casey/Shutterstock; 46 (CTR RT), Przemyslaw Wasilewski/Shutter-
stock; 46 (LOLE), JPL/NASA; 46 (LORT), JPL-Caltech/NASA; 47 (UPLE), Detlev van Ravenswaay/Science Source; 47 (UPRT),
DEA/D'ARCO EDITORI/De Agostini/Getty Images; 47 (CTR LE), Steve Gschmeissner/SPL/Getty Images; 47 (CTR RT),
Johan Swanepoel/Shutterstock; 47 (LOLE), David Aguilar/NGS; 47 (LORT), NASA

National Geographic supports K–12 educators with ELA Common Core Resources.
Visit natgeoed.org/commoncore for more information.

Printed in the United States of America
14/WOR/1

Table of Contents

Hey, Neighbor

Picture this: Pink skies. Orange sunsets. Vast deserts and massive canyons. You can see these sites and more . . . on Mars!

This planet is one of Earth's nearest neighbors in our solar system. But even though it's closer than other planets, Mars is still far away. It takes nine months to travel there in a spacecraft.

Mars Meaning

SOLAR SYSTEM: The collection of planets, their moons, and smaller rocky objects that circle a star

A space vehicle named Spirit took this photograph of the surface of Mars.

Our Solar System

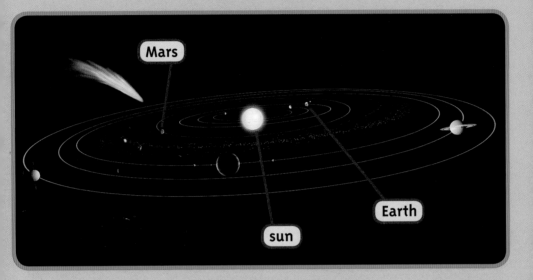

Mars

sun

Earth

Earth

Mars

Earth vs. Mars

	EARTH	MARS
Length of Day	24 hours	24 hours 37 minutes
Length of Year	365 Earth days	687 Earth days
Moons	One	Two
Average Temperature	59°F	-81°F
Diameter	7,926 miles	4,222 miles

Mars is the fourth planet from the sun. It's about half the size of Earth. Only the planet Mercury is smaller than Mars.

In some ways, Mars is very similar to our planet. Like Earth, Mars is a rocky planet. It has valleys and volcanoes, just like Earth does.

But there are also a lot of differences. For example, Mars spins more slowly on its axis than Earth does. As a result, a Mars day lasts 37 minutes longer than an Earth day.

These differences are part of what makes Mars so interesting. Mars has fascinated sky-watchers for thousands of years.

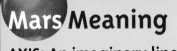

Mars Meaning

AXIS: An imaginary line that a planet rotates around

"Blood" in the Sky

More than 2,000 years ago, ancient Romans noticed a red glowing object when they gazed at the night sky. The planet's color reminded them of blood. So they named the planet Mars, after their god of war. The name stuck. Today, the nickname for Mars is the Red Planet.

Roman statue of Mars, the god of war

rusty car

The Red Planet's rosy color looks like rust. In a way, it is. The dusty soil on Mars contains iron. Iron is a metal and the main ingredient in rust. This makes Mars look like a ball of metal left out in the rain.

rusty can

This photograph, taken by the space vehicle Spirit, shows rocks in an area of Mars called Gusev Crater.

Extreme Planet

Red-colored Mars looks blazing hot. But it's actually freezing cold. It's farther from the warming sun than Earth is. Plus, its thin atmosphere isn't good at holding in heat.

Earth's thick atmosphere holds in the sun's heat like a blanket. But on Mars, most of the sun's heat bounces back into space.

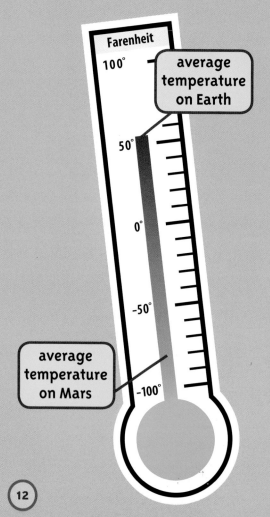

Farenheit

100°

average temperature on Earth

50°

0°

-50°

average temperature on Mars

-100°

Mars Meaning

ATMOSPHERE: The layer of gases that surrounds a planet

Researchers test space suits during a training session.

A Deadly Breath

Did you know that breathing the air on Mars would kill us? The atmosphere is made up of mostly carbon dioxide. That's the gas we breathe out. Earth's atmosphere is made mostly of nitrogen and oxygen, the gas we need to breathe. Since there's no oxygen on Mars, visitors there would have to wear a space suit that supplies oxygen. The outfit you pack for Mars would literally mean life or death!

If that doesn't make you want to pass on a ticket to Mars, consider this. Planetwide dust storms sometimes blanket Mars for months.

This illustration shows a Martian dust storm over the Gusev Crater area.

Frozen carbon dioxide, or dry ice, forms frost and falls as snow on Mars!

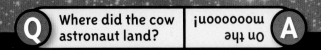
In addition, tornadoes of dust called dust devils often swirl over the surface. They can reach heights of 3,000 feet. Dust devils form all the time.

5 Cool Things About Mars

Olympus Mons on Mars

1

Mount Everest on Earth

Mars is home to the tallest volcano in the solar system. This volcano, called Olympus Mons, is three times as high as Mount Everest!

2

This illustration shows how water could have flooded Mars.

Some scientists think that 3.5 billion years ago, floods on Mars made huge river channels. The channels are visible from space today.

3

Grand Canyon

Mars has a canyon that's over four times as deep as the Grand Canyon. It would stretch from New York to San Francisco.

4

summer on Earth

Mars has four seasons. They're much longer than the seasons on Earth. Earth's summer is 94 days. Summer on Mars is 199!

5

Mars, along with Mercury, has the lowest surface gravity in the solar system. If you weigh 100 pounds on Earth, you'd only weigh 38 pounds on Mars!

Mars Meaning

GRAVITY: An invisible force that pulls objects toward each other

A Watery Past

Today, liquid water probably can't exist on the surface of Mars. The atmosphere is too thin. The temperature is too cold. All the water on Mars is frozen solid in the north and south poles or under the ground.

But this wasn't always the case. Scientists think water flowed on Mars after the planet formed. There might even have been large oceans and rivers.

Why does this matter? Water is necessary for life to exist. If it flowed on Mars, maybe life existed there too. But how can we find out?

Layers of ice are exposed in a cliff in the north polar region of Mars.

Computer artwork shows what rivers on Mars might have looked like 3.5 billion years ago.

Next Stop, Mars!

The best way to find out if liquid water—or life—was ever on Mars is to pay the planet a visit. For the past 50 years, scientists have been doing just that … except that spacecraft, not humans, have been making the trip.

Check out some major milestones in Mars exploration.

1964

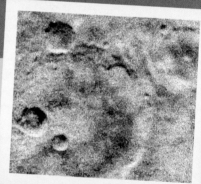

Mariner 4, a small space probe, flew past Mars. It took the first photographs of the planet's surface.

1975

Viking 1 was the first American spacecraft to land on Mars. It took photos and climate measurements for seven years.

1996

Sojourner was the first robotic rover on Mars.

Spirit

2004

Spirit and Opportunity are twin rovers that have taken thousands of photos and measurements. Spirit shut down in 2010. Opportunity continues to send information back to Earth.

2008

Phoenix Mars Lander found evidence of snow falling in clouds on Mars.

2012

Curiosity began its planned two-year mission. It's a rover that's like a science lab on wheels. It's looking for evidence that life could have existed on Mars.

Curiosity's high-tech camera is on its robotic arm.

Mars Meaning

PROBE: A spacecraft with no one on board. It gathers information in space and sends it back to Earth.

ROVER: A wheeled vehicle that explores another planet with scientific instruments. Scientists control it from Earth.

Early spacecraft were made of the best technology available at the time. Still, they were simple compared to what we send to Mars today. Mariner 4 returned only 22 photographs of the surface of Mars.

Later spacecraft were able to send thousands of photographs. These more advanced spacecraft were like two vehicles in one. Viking 1 had two parts—an orbiter and a lander. The lander touched down on Mars. The orbiter stayed in orbit around the planet.

Mars Meaning

ORBIT: A circular path around a planet, star, moon, or asteroid

drawing of Curiosity

Rovers are the most complex Mars explorers yet. They roll over the surface taking pictures, soil samples, and measurements.

Cruising With Curiosity

Curiosity is the largest and most advanced rover sent to Mars. It landed there in August 2012. The car-size rover is helping scientists study the Red Planet in more detail than ever before. Its mission was scheduled to last 23 months, but it will likely be extended.

Curiosity's job is to look for water—or evidence that water used to be there—in the rocks and soil on Mars. It's also looking for habitats where living things could have lived. To do this, Curiosity uses 17 high-tech cameras, a rock-zapping laser, and a nuclear-powered laboratory.

Mars Meaning

HABITAT: The area where a living thing makes its home

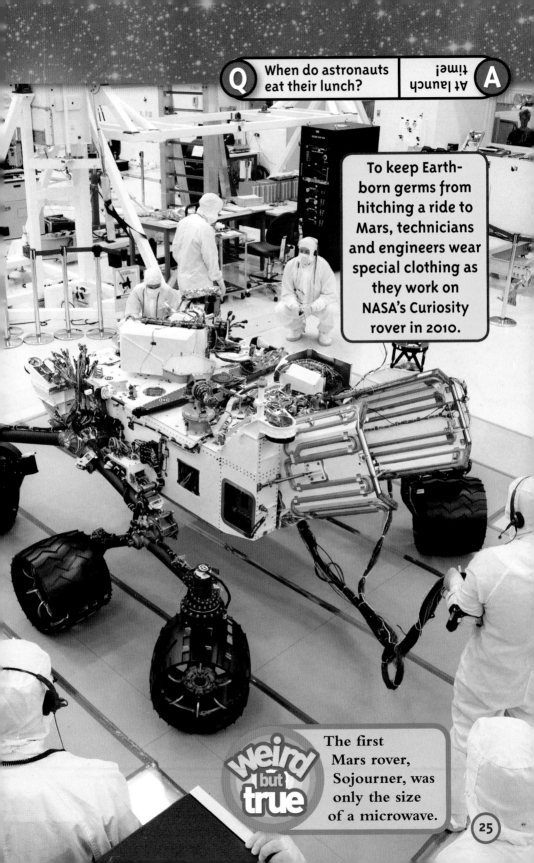

To keep Earth-born germs from hitching a ride to Mars, technicians and engineers wear special clothing as they work on NASA's Curiosity rover in 2010.

weird but true

The first Mars rover, Sojourner, was only the size of a microwave.

Engineers on Earth control Curiosity's movements. After Curiosity landed on Mars, members of the control team switched to Martian time for three months. This helped them monitor the mission more easily.

A simple math mistake could have been the cause of a Mars mission failure in 1999.

Flight director David Oh's son Devyn shows a sign on his front door that reads: "Flight Director Asleep on Mars Time, Come Back Later."

The family of one flight director, David Oh, spent an entire summer on Mars time, too. After three weeks, their schedule was turned completely upside down. They sometimes went to bed at noon and went bike riding at 3 a.m!

David Oh's son Braden peeks through sealed bedroom windows. The sunlight was blocked so the family could sleep on Mars time.

A Long Journey

So far, scientists have only sent robots to Mars. But one day, they want to send people. Experts have different ideas on the best way to travel to Mars. But one thing is for sure: These types of missions to Mars would likely take years to complete.

The journey itself would take about nine months. Once there, astronauts would likely have to set up areas to work, live, and grow their own food. To go outside, they would have to put on space suits. Talking to people at home would be difficult. Communication signals would take up to 20 minutes to reach Earth.

A rocket carrying the Maven spacecraft blasts off at Cape Canaveral Air Force Station, Florida, U.S.A., in 2013. Maven will collect information on the atmosphere of Mars.

To meet the challenges, groups of scientists have created Mars-mission training grounds. They set up fake space stations so crews can practice surviving on the Red Planet.

Two scientists perform a training mission in Hanksville, Utah, U.S.A.

Bases are often located in dry, empty areas that look like Mars, like the top of a Hawaiian volcano or a field in the Canadian Arctic. Scientists hope to learn how to make a real-life Mars mission successful.

Dr. Robert Howard checks a vegetable-growing experiment. This food would be grown by astronauts far away from Earth.

Since Mars doesn't have supermarkets, astronauts will have to prepare and grow their own food. Scientists are studying what astronauts will eat when they're 150 million miles from Earth.

Food brought from Earth will require at least a three-year shelf life. But the food will also need to be nutritious so Mars travelers don't get sick. And a variety of food will help keep them from getting bored.

Astronauts might be able to grow plants like strawberries and tomatoes in a greenhouse. Fresh fruits and veggies would be a welcome treat.

Pepperoni, Please!

No pizza delivery on Mars? No problem! Astronauts on Mars may be able to "print" a pie with a 3-D printer. Scientists are working on a device that makes food with ingredients like flavored powders, water, and oil with the push of a button.

Your Body in Space

Before you pack your bags for Mars, you should know that living in space can have some wild effects on the human body. Why? Our bodies are suited for life on Earth. We're used to having the force of gravity constantly tugging on our bones and muscles.

Without gravity's strong pull, some body systems start to go haywire.

✓ Muscles get weaker.

✓ Bones can break easily.

✓ Fluid builds up at the top of the body, making the face puffy and the legs look shrunken.

✓ Headaches and stomachaches result from space sickness, a type of motion sickness.

During space travel, the pull of Earth's gravity gets weaker the farther you get from the planet. Until a spacecraft reaches Mars and is under the pull of that planet's gravity, objects float in a state of weightlessness.

Fortunately, exercise and a special diet can control some of these effects.

Astronaut Sunita Williams is tied to the treadmill so she won't float away.

Space Race!

Astronaut Sunita Williams completed a triathlon in space! She ran on a treadmill, cycled on a stationary bike, and "swam" using a special exercise machine. She did it all while aboard the International Space Station!

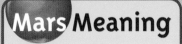

Mars Meaning

WEIGHTLESSNESS: The sensation of floating in space

Greening the Red Planet?

One day, humans might be able to live on Mars. But it would take a lot of time and effort to make the Red Planet into a place people could live. The process of making a place more Earth-like is called terraforming. Here's how humans imagine we might someday be able to turn Mars into a "new" Earth in 1,000 years with future technology.

An Idea for Making Mars Earth-Like

YEAR ZERO

The project might begin with a series of missions to set up living quarters.

YEAR 100

Human-built factories could
spew powerful greenhouse gases
to boost Mars's atmosphere.
The greenhouse gas buildup would
begin to warm the frozen planet.

Over time, Mars could look
more like Earth.

YEAR 200

Rain would fall and water would
flow once enough greenhouse
gases had been released.
Simple microbes and plant life
could start growing on rocks.

YEAR 600

Microbes would create organic soil and add oxygen to the atmosphere. Humans could introduce flowering plants and evergreen forests to see if they would grow.

YEAR 1,000

Since oxygen levels would remain low, humans on Mars would require oxygen tanks to breathe outside. Energy for cities might come from nuclear power and wind turbines.

Meet a Martian!

Mars has long held a special place in people's imaginations. In books, television, and movies, Martians are often shown as little green men. The idea that aliens live on Mars began more than 100 years ago.

In the late 1800s, some astronomers claimed to see channels on the surface of Mars through their telescopes. They believed that the channels were canals. They thought that Martians built the canals to transport water to cities. The canals, it turns out, don't exist. But the idea that Mars might have advanced life-forms remained. Today, we know that's not the case.

Mars Meaning

ASTRONOMERS: Scientists who study objects in space

The book *Mars* by Percival Lowell was published in 1895.

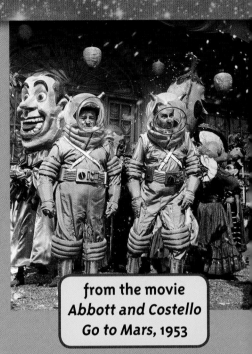

from the movie *Abbott and Costello Go to Mars*, 1953

The 1898 novel *War of the Worlds* by H. G. Wells was the first story about a Martian invasion.

1938 movie poster

Martian toy

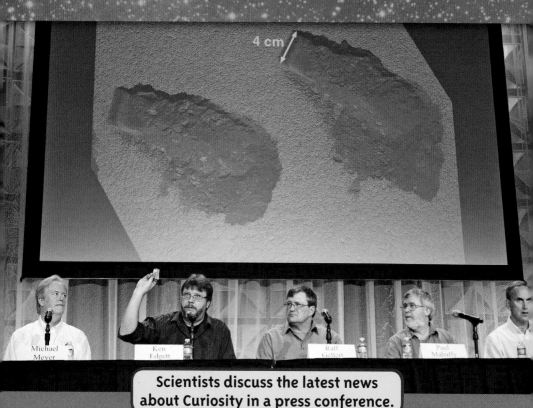

4 cm

Michael
Meyer

Ken
Edgett

Ralf
Gellert

Paul
Mahaffy

Scientists discuss the latest news
about Curiosity in a press conference.

It's fun to think about what an imaginary
Martian might look like. And it's neat to
dream about living on a green, terraformed
Mars in the future. But scientists are most
interested in knowing if life ever existed
on Mars in the past. Many believe there is
a strong chance it did. What would this life
have looked like?

It probably would look like the microbe in the photo below, which is too small to be seen without a microscope. If that's true, then real Martians are just like creatures that are all around us here on Earth.

Mars Meaning

MICROBE: A simple, single-celled creature that is too small to be seen by the naked eye

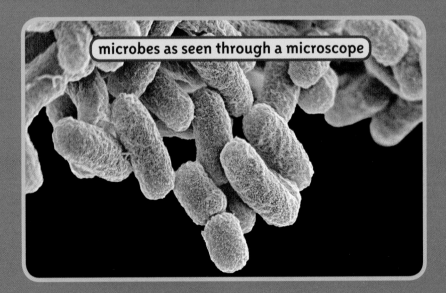

microbes as seen through a microscope

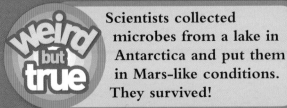

weird but true

Scientists collected microbes from a lake in Antarctica and put them in Mars-like conditions. They survived!

Be a Quiz Whiz!

How much do you know about Mars? After reading this book, probably a lot! Take this quiz and find out.

Answers at the bottom of page 45.

Mars is the _____ planet from the sun.
A. Second
B. Fourth
C. Sixth
D. Last

What substance gives Mars its red color?
A. Carbon
B. Sulfur
C. Granite
D. Iron

The climate on Mars is _____ than Earth's.
A. Colder
B. Hotter
C. Not very different
D. Wetter

Which characteristic does Mars currently NOT share with Earth?
A. Seasons
B. Volcanoes
C. Mountains
D. Liquid water

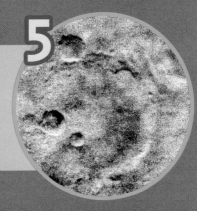

Which spacecraft took the first photos of Mars?
A. Curiosity
B. Spirit
C. Sojourner
D. Mariner 4

What happens to objects in a state of weightlessness?
A. They sink.
B. They float.
C. They fly.
D. They move in circles.

Which is a requirement for any food brought to Mars?
A. It's spicy.
B. It's colorful.
C. It doesn't spoil quickly.
D. It doesn't need to be prepared.

Glossary

ASTRONOMERS: Scientists who study objects in space

GRAVITY: An invisible force that pulls objects toward each other

HABITAT: The area where a living thing makes its home

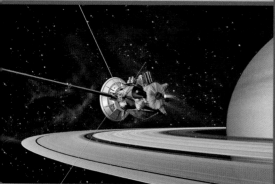

PROBE: A spacecraft with no one on board. It gathers information in space and sends it back to Earth.

ROVER: A wheeled vehicle that explores another planet with scientific instruments. Scientists control it from Earth.

ATMOSPHERE: The layer of gases that surrounds a planet

AXIS: An imaginary line that a planet rotates around

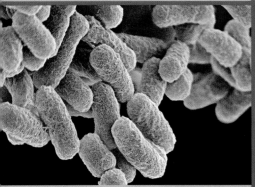

MICROBE: A simple, single-celled creature that is too small to be seen by the naked eye

ORBIT: A circular path around a planet, star, moon, or asteroid

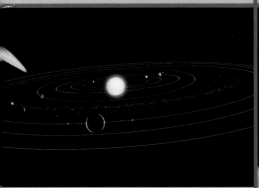

SOLAR SYSTEM: The collection of planets, their moons, and smaller rocky objects that circle a star

WEIGHTLESSNESS: The sensation of floating in space

Index